INSIDE

Philip Osment

INSIDE

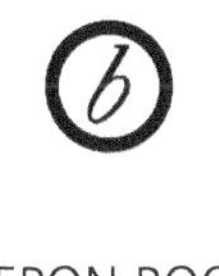

OBERON BOOKS
LONDON

First published in 2010 by Oberon Books Ltd
521 Caledonian Road, London N7 9RH
Tel: 020 7607 3637 / Fax: 020 7607 3629
e-mail: info@oberonbooks.com
www.oberonbooks.com

A catalogue record for this book is available from the British Library.

ISBN: 978-1-84943-023-4

Cover photography by Jonathan Birch

Introduction

In 2007 Jim Pope asked me to come and work with his group of NEETs (young people not in education, employment or training) at the National Youth Theatre. This group were taking part in the Playing Up course which Jim had set up as part of an outreach programme run by the NYT. The young people involved had dropped out of education and some had experiences of homelessness, probation or prison.

At the same time Jim was conducting workshops in young offenders institutes (YOIs) as part of this outreach programme and he invited me to participate in the one he was running with a young fathers' group in Rochester Prison which houses convicted sentenced young offenders serving up to six years. The young men had previously all participated in a programme called Fathers Inside run by an organisation called Safeground.

Paul Roseby, the Artistic Director of the NYT had at the same time proposed that I should be commissioned to write a play entitled *Fathers Inside* and on the basis of this and my experiences of the workshop in the prison, Jim and I began work with the members of the Playing Up course in February 2008. Their initial task was to create characters who, for some reason, were incarcerated and had young children. These characters came out of discussions we had about my experiences in Rochester and out of their own experiences and knowledge. We began to "hotseat" the characters – interviewing them about their lives which helped to define who they were and what the relationships between them might be. These relationships were further developed through improvisation and slowly a story emerged. This process culminated in three improvised performances in the Studio at the Soho Theatre in May 2008. A few weeks later we took this improvised version to Cookham Wood YOI where the young men in the audience were rapt throughout and talked eagerly about the issues that the play brought up for them. Most importantly they wanted to talk to the actors about their journeys – how they came to be such accomplished actors.

In 2009 our cast began the final year of the Playing Up programme – an accredited A-level standard course which would qualify them for higher education. It was decided that as their final presentation our actors would perform *Fathers Inside.* I scripted the play and it had a longer run in the studio at the Soho Theatre in late August and early September 2009, garnering enthusiastic reviews and responses.

Given this positive response, Jim and I decided to set up a company (Playing On) to provide professional development and employment for our actors. We made an Arts Council application to restage a reworked version of the play which we now called *Inside* to avoid confusion with the Safeground programme and to research a new project with our cast. At this point the Roundhouse came on board with the offer of financial support and a run in their studio theatre.

Philip Osment, October 2010

PLAYING ON

Co directors: Jim Pope and Philip Osment
Company registration number: 07260538
ITC registered members
81 Chestnut Road
London SE27 9LD
07812 241882

Characters

LIAM
(40s white, workshop leader)

DOM
(20 black British, Liam's assistant)

Prisoners:

OLU
(20 Nigerian)

JAMAL
(19 black British)

ASWAN
(19 black British)

DAMIAN
(19 Afro Carribbean)

BROWNIE
(20 black British)

TOMMY
(19 white)

HASAN
(18 Turkish British)

Inside by Philip Osment was produced by Playing On, in association with the Roundhouse. It was first performed on Friday 12th of November 2010 at the Roundhouse Studio Theatre with the following cast:

LIAM, Jim Pope
DOM, Andre Skeete
OLU, Ayo Bodunrin
DAMIAN, Kyle Thorne
JAMAL, Michael Amaning
ASWAN, Darren Douglas
BROWNIE, Segun Olaiya
TOMMY, Jacob James Beswick
HASAN, Tarkan Cetinkaya

Directed by Jim Pope and Philip Osment
Producer Talita Moffatt
Design Michael Breakey
Lighting Ian Scott
Sound Paul Millen
Production Manager Greg Piggott
Stage Manager Beth Hoare-Barnes
Production Assistant Hana Tait
Assistant to the Producer Kasia Nossier

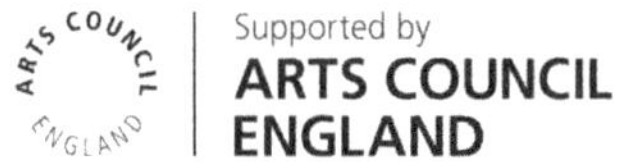

Thanks to Brett Smith, Mozzam Ghazzi, Claudio Barbosa,Will Cardoza, Tom Kirkin, Adrian Felix Njenga Jnr, Adam Williamson, Daniel Ward, Nathan Ives-Moiba, Anna Niland, Isobel Hawson, Paul Roseby and to Sonia Franklin-Smith at Rochester Prison.

SCENE ONE - THE FIRST CLASS

The young men and the workshop leaders sit in a circle. LIAM, OLU, JAMAL, ASWAN, DAMIAN, DOM, BROWNIE, TOMMY and HASAN.

DAMIAN has his arm around ASWAN – they are close and knew each other before they came to prison. ASWAN, DAMIAN and JAMAL all wear prison issue crucifixes.

OLU: My name is Olu and I have four children. Two boys and two girls.

DAMIAN: Four?

OLU: The girls are called Kiera and Lateesha and the boys are Tobi and Cameron.

DAMIAN: How did that happen, blud?

OLU: How do you think?

DAMIAN: How old are you?

OLU: Twenty.

DAMIAN: All with the same baby mother?

OLU: Yes.

DAMIAN: For real?

JAMAL: Bullshit.

LIAM: Let's move on, can we?

DAMIAN: *(In response to "Bullshit".)* What?

JAMAL: It's four different mothers.

DAMIAN: That true?

BROWNIE: He's a sex machine.

OLU: Huh?

BROWNIE: In his culture men have loads of wives.

OLU: What?

BROWNIE: He's from Africa – that's why he talks like that.

He imitates OLU.

LIAM: Let's move on.

OLU: Ah yes. Very funny.

JAMAL: How many kids you got Brownie?

BROWNIE: Loads mate. One of them was with your missus.

LIAM: Let's keep going round the circle. What about you?

JAMAL: I got a daughter that's two –

LIAM: Say your name and then what kids you've got.

JAMAL: My name's Jamal and I got a daughter that's two.

BROWNIE points to himself indicating that it's his daughter.

JAMAL: What's your problem?

BROWNIE: Nothing mate.

LIAM: *(Indicating ASWAN.)* Next?

JAMAL: His missus hasn't popped it yet.

DAMIAN: What? Oh yeah.

JAMAL: Gonna be a Daddy soon he is.

He reaches out and rubs ASWAN's head roughly but affectionately. DAMIAN still has his arm around ASWAN.

ASWAN: Yeah, my name's Aswan and I got a six-month yeah on the way.

LIAM: Congratulations.

ASWAN: Three months to go you know.

LIAM: Do you know what it's going to be?

ASWAN: No, have to sort that with the missis innit?

DAMIAN: Sweet.

LIAM: Exciting time for you.

ASWAN: Yeah.

LIAM: So moving on.

He looks at DAMIAN.

DAMIAN: What?

LIAM: Say your name and what kids you've got.

DAMIAN: They know my name.

LIAM: I don't.

DAMIAN: My name's Damian.

DAMIAN thinks he's finished. He looks at LIAM who is still looking at him.

DAMIAN: What?

LIAM: You have children?

DAMIAN: Yeah.

LIAM: So tell us how many, how old and what their names are.

DAMIAN: I got a boy. He's eleven months.

LIAM: OK and he's called?

BROWNIE: Fuck's sake!

LIAM: Alright!

DAMIAN: What's your problem, blud?

BROWNIE: Just give us his name!

LIAM: OK Brownie. Is that right, "Brownie"?

BROWNIE: Yeah.

LIAM: So what's your boy called, Damian?

DAMIAN: Connor.

LIAM: Thank you. Next?

BROWNIE: What about you, Liam? You got kids?

LIAM: Yes I have. I have a boy – he's eight. His name is Zach.

OLU: *(Repeating the name to see what it feels like.)* Zack!

BROWNIE: What sort of name's that?

OLU: Zack!

ASWAN: Short for Zachary, ain't it?

LIAM: That's right. Anyway.

We have reached DOM's place in the circle.

DOM: Yeah, my name's Dom and I haven't got any kids.

BROWNIE: So what's he doing here?

LIAM: Dom and I are running the sessions with you.

DAMIAN: Are we going to do some drama?

LIAM: Yes we are.

DAMIAN: When are we going to do it?

LIAM: Well this is part of it.

ASWAN: Yeah guv told me that we gonna be able to ask like our families to come and watch us at the end.

LIAM: That's right, we're going to make a piece of theatre and then at the end of the two weeks there's going to be a performance in the chapel and as long as you're allowed visitors you can ask your families.

DAMIAN: Sick.

ASWAN: Cos I need to let my missis know if she's gonna come.

LIAM: So you need to get your requests in as soon as you can. But can we move on?

BROWNIE: So how's Dom gonna teach us if he ain't got no kids?

LIAM: That's a good point. We're not really here to teach you. We're going to learn from each other about being a parent and things you might want to do with your children, how you might want to be with them.

ASWAN: Yeah, but like this guy ain't got no kids.

DOM: But it's something I aspire to.

BROWNIE: What?

JAMAL: Brownie don't understand words like that.

DOM: It's one of my ambitions.

BROWNIE: Ambitions?

DOM: To become a father.

Uproar from the lads.

DAMIAN: Get a little grind going.

ASWAN: It ain't hard.

BROWNIE: Mine was really hard when I fucked your missis.

LIAM: OK, that's it. We're not going to get anywhere unless we respect each other. Later we're going to agree some rules – because we won't be able to make a piece of theatre if there's no respect. But for the moment, Brownie, can I ask you not to disrespect each other.

BROWNIE: You was saying Dom.

OLU: *(Saying the name just for the sake of saying it.)* Dom.

LIAM: He was saying that he wants to raise a child at some point.

BROWNIE: You got a girlfriend, Dom?

LIAM: Brownie mate, we're not here to share everything about our personal lives.

TOMMY: It's what you're asking us to do.

LIAM: Pardon?

BROWNIE: That's right.

TOMMY: Why should we tell you stuff if he's not prepared to?

DOM: I've got a partner.

LIAM: Right. So Brownie? You got children?

BROWNIE: Yeah I got Archie.

LIAM: And how old is Archie?

BROWNIE: Three.

LIAM: Nice one. And you?

TOMMY: I'm Tommy. My little girl's called Emily. She's two.

LIAM: Thank you, Tommy.

TOMMY: You're welcome.

LIAM: And lastly.....

BROWNIE: He's just come in here. He's called Hasan.

LIAM: Let him speak for himself.

HASAN: I'm Hasan. I got a girl. A daughter. She's three weeks. Four weeks.

LIAM: Four weeks! Wow! And her name?

HASAN: Candy.

JAMAL, ASWAN and DAMIAN snigger at the name.

DAMIAN: Where are you from, blud?

HASAN: East London.

DAMIAN: Oh yeah, which bit?

LIAM: Fascinating as it is to find out where you're all from, it's not the point of today. Our aim is to get you thinking about what it is to be a father and what your child needs from you.

OLU: A father must provide for his children.

JAMAL, ASWAN and DAMIAN laugh.

OLU: I give my children money.

LIAM: Good, but we're also talking about emotional needs your children might have.

OLU: They have everything they need.

LIAM: That's admirable, Olu.

DAMIAN: Sir?

LIAM: I'm Liam.

DAMIAN: We gonna do the drama ting now? I wanna do some acting.

SCENE TWO – ON THE WING – VOICES 1

DAMIAN: Hey, Aswan. Aswan!

ASWAN: What?

BROWNIE: Shut the fuck up!

DAMIAN: Aswan!

ASWAN: What?

DAMIAN: You get your VO?

ASWAN: She's coming in at the end of the week.

JAMAL: He's gonna be getting some TLC.

ASWAN: That's right.

BROWNIE: Jamal's missis is a slag.

JAMAL: Fuck off, Brownie.

OLU: Be quiet please. I'm praying.

He isn't praying.

BRO/DAM/JAM/ASW: Shut up Olu!

BROWNIE: Fucking raghead!

SCENE THREE — ASSOCIATION

The Gym.

BROWNIE is skipping – HASAN is watching and TOMMY is doing sit-ups.

BROWNIE: You can't hide in your cell all the time, mate. Alright, the food's shit, there's no women and the rooms are too small. But you can't let it get to you. You gotta get out and show them wankers that you don't give a shit about them. Lot of wankers in here. Screws are wankers, most of the other cons are wankers, the chaplain's a wanker, governor's a wanker. So you have to find the people who don't spend all their time with their hands around their dicks, or their hands around someone else's dick. You stick with me and Tommy. We got a way of getting through. You gotta be strong, mate. Yeah?

HASAN: Yeah.

BROWNIE: I mean that's not just about coming to the gym and doing weights. I'm talking about being mentally strong. Look at this guy. He don't exactly look like Arnold Schwarzenegger. But he's mentally strong. Don't take no shit, do you Tommy?

TOMMY: No.

BROWNIE: The stuff this guy reads. He's like a fucking professor.

HASAN: Right.

BROWNIE: He's teaching me all sorts of stuff, ain't you Tommy? Meditation, Zen fucking Buddhism, fucking philosophy. Who was that kraut your were reading the other day, Tommy?

TOMMY: Eckhart Tolle.

BROWNIE: That's right. This guy says you gotta just focus on the here and now. That's what I'm doing when I'm skipping – I'm not thinking about tomorrow, or next week, or next month or next year, or what happens when I fucking die. That's all about wanting something that's not here. You gotta just focus on now – that's right isn't it Tommy?

TOMMY: That's right.

BROWNIE: See my Dad? He was always in and out of prison.

HASAN: Yeah?

BROWNIE: Fucking great role model, he was. I remember him saying that the killer was, if you thought about how much time you still had left to do. He said it drove you mad. He got ten years for aggravated burglary last time he was in. Poor fucker. How long have you got?

HASAN shrugs.

BROWNIE: Don't you know? You been sentenced, ain't you?

HASAN: Yeah. Six months.

TOMMY: What did you do? Murder somebody?

This makes BROWNIE laugh.

BROWNIE: Fucking Tommy. You crack me up man.

HASAN looks uncomfortable as BROWNIE laughs at TOMMY's joke.

BROWNIE: Be in the moment, that's the answer. Isn't that right, Tommy?

TOMMY: That's right Brownie.

BROWNIE: That's where Shirley comes in.

HASAN: Who?

BROWNIE: *(Stopping skipping and holding up the rope.)* She's slim, petite and you can jump all over her.

HASAN: Right.

BROWNIE: Me and Shirley spend hours together just being in the present. You can have a go with her if you like. Here.

He hands HASAN the rope.

SCENE FOUR – ASSOCIATION AROUND THE POOL TABLE

DAMIAN: Boom, rack 'em!

ASWAN is racking the balls.

JAMAL: Me and you against Aswan and him.

DAMIAN: I'm playing with Aswan.

JAMAL: Alright. Come on, raghead.

OLU: I'll break.

JAMAL: No, I'll break.

DAMIAN: We gonna put some burn on the table?

JAMAL: Or p's.

DAMIAN: Burn.

JAMAL breaks and expresses disgust at his bad luck.

DAMIAN: Go Aswan.

ASWAN sizes up his shot.

JAMAL: That fucking Brownie. His head's gonna get opened up.

DAMIAN: He's baiting you.

ASWAN has shot.

DAMIAN: Shot blud. We're spots.

ASWAN lines up another shot.

JAMAL: I never thought Brownie would do the drama ting. I wouldn't have done it meself if I thought he was going to do it.

DAMIAN: Perhaps he wants to be an actor.

The others laugh.

ASWAN: It was probably Tommy's idea.

JAMAL: Fucking nonce.

DAMIAN: Who?

JAMAL: Tommy.

ASWAN: He's trying to educate Brownie.

They laugh again.

JAMAL: Brownie can't even read.

DAMIAN: *(To ASWAN about his playing.)* Yes my son!

JAMAL: This drama ting is shit. Zip, zap, boing! How did it go, Olu?

OLU: Huh?

JAMAL: *(Imitating OLU by moving his hips suggestively on the boing.)* Boing.

The others crack up.

JAMAL: It's fucking gay!

DAMIAN: That Liam's been on The Bill.

JAMAL: So?

DAMIAN: I wouldn't mind that.

JAMAL: We ain't doing the Bill though. I ain't saying shit about my kid. Not with the fucking screws listening to everything. And that fucking Tommy.

OLU: Tommy. Tommy!

JAMAL: *(To ASWAN who is sizing up his next shot.)* You playing or what?

OLU: Tommy is very clever.

JAMAL: Bullshit. Fucking nonce. You see the way he looks at you? Like you're a fucking piece of shit. Just because he's got Brownie's protection.

ASWAN misses his shot.

OLU: Yes! My go.

ASWAN and DAMIAN slap hands and DAMIAN stands with his arm around ASWAN.

JAMAL: I'm going to shank that nonce one day.

ASWAN: No-one will touch him. They're shook.

JAMAL: I'm not shook. You saying I'm shook? Brownie don't frighten me.

DAMIAN: Jamal goes to Tommy's cell when he first came in here and tries to tax him and Tommy just gives him lip and then Brownie comes in and tells Jamal to fuck off. Oh my days.

DAMIAN and ASWAN laugh.

OLU pots a ball.

OLU: Yes.

He does a victory dance.

DAMIAN: That's one of ours. You're circles blud.

JAMAL: You tramp!

OLU: I thought we was spots.

DAMIAN: *(Taking the cue.)* Two goes to us.

JAMAL: One day when Brownie's not looking, I'm gonna get that nonce. Fucking kiddy fiddler.

SCENE FIVE – THE SECOND CLASS

The class are sitting in rows and OLU is standing before them.

OLU: But I want to sing a song. I am a good singer.

LIAM: Maybe later, Olu.

OLU: So what do you want me to do, eh?

LIAM: What do you want for your child – or in your case, your children and what would you be prepared to give up so that they can have it?

OLU: What do I want for my child? My children have everything. I work hard to make sure they have everything.

LIAM: You work hard?

OLU: Yes.

LIAM: What work do you do, Olu?

BROWNIE: Dealing.

OLU: I get money for my baby mothers.

LIAM: I see. How do you get it?

OLU looks at him and starts to laugh.

LIAM: It's a serious question, Olu. Cos if the way you earn your money lands you in here then you can't really say that you're providing for your kids, can you? What could you give up to be able to spend time with your kids and be a father for them?

OLU: Ok Ok. I want my children to be rich and I will not come to prison.

LIAM: And how are you going to stop coming to prison?

OLU: I don't get caught.

The others laugh and hoot.

LIAM: Quiet, quiet. So what you're saying is that you're not prepared to give up crime for your kids.

OLU: No. Yes. I give up crime. I'll be a good boy.

LIAM: Well, think about it Olu. OK give him a clap.

Some applause.

LIAM: Who's next?

BROWNIE: Is that all you want us to do?

LIAM: Yes, Brownie. But think about what it will mean on Friday week when your family, your partners, your kids, your parents, your siblings, whoever –

DAMIAN: What's siblings?

LIAM: Your brothers and sisters. All those people sitting there listening to you say these things. Think what it will make them feel.

BROWNIE: Sick.

LIAM: Thank you Brownie.

DAMIAN: So aren't we going to do any acting?

LIAM: Yes, we're going to listen to this and then we're going to do some little dramas about them. So do you want to do one?

DAMIAN: What?

BROWNIE: I don't.

LIAM: *(To DAMIAN.)* Are you going to say something?

DAMIAN: What do you want me to say?

LIAM: Get on stage first. I thought you wanted to act.

DAMIAN: I do.

LIAM: So get up.

DAMIAN: Yeah.

He stands up in front of the class and looks at them. LIAM looks at him.

LIAM: Well?

DAMIAN: What?

LIAM: Go on.

DAMIAN: What do you want me to do?

LIAM: You're going to say what you want for Connor.

DAMIAN: Yeah.

He's still looking at LIAM for guidance.

LIAM: And?

DAMIAN: What in life?

LIAM: Yes.

DAMIAN: I think that's a conversation I'd have when he's older, so I could find out what he wants, you know, and then I just wanna support him, give him confidence.

Some of the others are laughing.

LIAM: Yeah, don't worry about them.

DAMIAN: *(To BROWNIE.)* What's funny, bruv?

LIAM: Dom, can you……?

He indicates that DOM should sit with BROWNIE, TOMMY and HASAN to stop them laughing.

DOM: Just keep it down lads.	LIAM: Don't worry about them. You're bigger than that.

BROWNIE: What?

DOM: Listen to him.

BROWNIE: Sorry Miss.

What I'm hearing is that you want Connor to have choices.

DAMIAM: Yeah, that's right.

LIAM: So what would you be prepared to give up in order for him to have choices

BROWNIE: Smoking crack.

DAMIAN: Who smokes crack, bruv?

LIAM: If a person did then I'm sure it would be a good thing to give up.

DAMIAN: What you saying? I don't smoke crack, nor nothing, man.

LIAM: So what is the thing you'd be prepared to give up?

BROWNIE is whispering to TOMMY.

DAMIAN: If I had to give up something…then I'll give up….

(To Brownie.)

Shut up. I'll give up like shotting, what got me in here, like selling drugs and 'at.

LIAM: OK. Yeah. So you want Connor to have choices. In order for him to have that you'll give up selling weed. I like that. That's good.

BROWNIE: Liam? What do you want? For your kid?

LIAM: What do I want? I want him to have empathy.

BROWNIE: What's that mean?

LIAM: It means that I want him to have understanding about other people and in order for that to happen I'll give up a few late nights on the sauce. I'll give him my quality time.

DAMIAN: On the sauce?

LIAM: Yeah, you know, going out.

BROWNIE: You an alcoholic, Liam?

LIAM: No. I'm a workaholic actually so maybe I should say I'll give up working too many hours.

BROWNIE: How much do you drink a night?

LIAM: Who's next? Jamal?

BROWNIE: How much do you drink?

JAMAL: I haven't got anything.

DAMIAN: Go on man. He's written something,

JAMAL: I got some lyrics.

LIAM: You can do that.

BROWNIE: He's not going to rap, is he? Fucking hell!

JAMAL: Don't let him take the piss out of me.

LIAM: Rise above it. Be bigger than that. Go on. You're on stage at Wembley arena and he's someone in the front row giving you jip.

BROWNIE: Just get on with it. Give him a beat, Tommy.

JAMAL: Shut up yeah?

LIAM: Rise above it. Come on Jamal.

JAMAL: If I went to jail, would you come and see me?
You say yes but your word might not be
reliable like handing out a CV.
Would you take the time to find out where I be?
If I wrote you a letter, would you reply?
You say yes, but would you really find the time?
Are you really my boy or girl?
Would you take care of things until I got out?
Seems like a lot to commit
but if we're down you won't have problems with it.
You can't be my friend one day then bounce the next
Cause I'm not rolling with that
You say you got chat
About how you got my back
But when it comes to the letters you might not wanna write back

ASWAN: Brrrrrup, brrrup. Yes that's lyrics J.

JAMAL finishes the last few lines unheard over the applause.

BROWNIE: That was fucking wicked, yeah?

JAMAL: He's taking the piss, man.

LIAM: Who you going to believe? He thought it was great, he's taking the piss.

DOM: It was great. Well done, Jamal.

JAMAL looks at DOM like he is the last person from whom he would want praise.

ASWAN: Here listen, Liam. Do you know, I gonna have to go next. I got a VO coming up innit?

LIAM: Sorry?

JAMAL: He's gotta go. His missis is coming to see him.

LIAM: Oh right, you should have said.

ASWAN: I wrote it last night, innit?

LIAM: Excellent. Let's hear it.

ASWAN: Yeah….Little man, –

BROWNIE: Brrrrup!

ASWAN: Here Liam, what's he doing man? Why you have to distract everybody, bruv? Just cool off.

BROWNIE: I didn't say nothing.

ASWAN: Little man, I know you're not here to see me in the flesh right now, but you truly are a blessing in disguise, brought to me to bring about a change and a purpose in my life. Son, I want you to be any and everything you wanna be. I want you to know that you'll always have a Dad that will be there for you to talk to, to play with, to learn, understand and feel close to. I want to provide you with things that I never had, to be shown love that I missed out on, to be given advice and confidence which I lacked at a young age. And hopefully to provide you with a little younger brother and sister so you don't feel lonely. When your Mother first told me she was pregnant….

BROWNIE: By Brownie.

Uproar. JAMAL and DAMIAN turn on BROWNIE.

BROWNIE: It just came out, man. I'm sorry for fuck's sake.

DAMIAN: Yeah go on, bruv, go on.

LIAM: Carry on.

ASWAN: I didn't wanna face the truth so I rejected you. Little did I know I was following in the same footsteps as my father when he had me. I was scared. Scared that I wouldn't be there for you, scared that I wasn't ready, scared that you'll grow up to be in the same position as I'm in now. But when I got the letter enclosed with the scan of your mother's womb, I cried, knowing I had something to feel proud of, a sense of fulfillment and determination to give you a life that you deserve. Little man, I know I'm gonna love you more than life itself and I'm gonna truly express it to the world. To guarantee your happiness, I would sacrifice my own.

BROWNIE: That's fucking beautiful.

DOM: That's brilliant.

BROWNIE: Fucking beautiful.

OLU: Now I do my song.

BROWNIE: There's no fucking singing.

DOM: Brownie!

BROWNIE: What?

ASWAN: Liam, I gotta go now.

LIAM: Ok, well done.

ASWAN goes and says his goodbyes to JAMAL and DAMIAN. They congratulate him.

DOM: Try not to shout everyone down.

BROWNIE whispers in TOMMY's ear about DOM being gay. DOM watches and tries not to let it get to him.

LIAM: See you tomorrow Aswan.

BROWNIE: Tell her I say hello.

ASWAN ignores him and goes.

OLU: So I do my song?

BROWNIE: There's no singing.

OLU: Yes. I got a very beautiful song.

LIAM: Hang on, Olu. Has anyone else got any statements they want to make before Olu does his song? Hasan?

HASAN looks terrified.

LIAM: Brownie, why don't you say something?

BROWNIE: I don't wanna say anything.

DAMIAN: Come on, Brownie, say something yeah!

JAMAL: He ain't got one.

BROWNIE: I got one.

LIAM: So did you write something?

JAMAL: He can't write Liam.

BROWNIE: I fucking got one. Shut up, man! Fuck's sake!

He reflects.

BROWNIE: I'll stay in here for the rest of my life if it means that Archie can have his dream.

Pause.

DAMIAN: Touching. Very touching.

Ironic applause.

DAMIAN: What would you give up?

BROWNIE: It's better than fucking rapping.

DAMIAN: What would he give up?

TOMMY: He's just told you. His life.

LIAM: Brownie mate, don't do down what other people have done.

BROWNIE: Liam, you're on their side.

LIAM: I'm not on anybody's side. But if you give it out you get it right back.

TOMMY whispers in BROWNIE's ear about this not being true.

OLU: So now, I sing.

LIAM: Yes, go on. We can have scenes, speeches, lyrics.

DAMIAN: Sir? You really a drama teacher?

BROWNIE: He's an alcoholic, aren't you Liam?

LIAM: Let's hear Olu's song.

BROWNIE: We've already heard it man.

LIAM: Come on, Olu.

OLU stands before them and sings.

SCENE SIX – LIAM AND DOM DEBRIEFING

DOM: It brings back stuff I thought I'd left behind, you know?

LIAM: What sort of stuff?

DOM: You know, getting bullied I suppose. I find myself watching them all the time to see if they're taking the piss. Just like school.

LIAM: Yeah, I know what you mean. You have to have a thick skin.

DOM: Yeah.

LIAM: But you have to remember that we walk out of here every night. They don't.

DOM: I know.

LIAM: I mean, look at Brownie. "I'll stay here forever if Archie can have his dream!" What's that about? He probably will be here forever. And Olu! That song. It was so shit!

They both laugh.

LIAM: I don't know if we can make much difference for them. But then you have to think about the effect we're having on guys like Aswan and Damian. Jamal even.

DOM: Yeah, Aswan's piece was amazing.

LIAM: And Damian cracks me up.

DOM: Yeah.

LIAM looks at his watch.

LIAM: So are you ok for tomorrow?

DOM: I guess.

LIAM: And you'll run that game with them?

DOM: Yeah.

LIAM: So are we done?

DOM: I'm finding Brownie a bit difficult to handle.

LIAM: I know what you mean. As soon as I said that about being on the sauce I could have bitten my tongue off.

DOM: He keeps making comments, you know?

LIAM: It's Tommy who's the really tricky one.

DOM: Mmmm.

LIAM: What sort of comments?

DOM: About my sexuality.

LIAM: Really? Well you know, you don't have to disclose what you don't feel comfortable disclosing. Some practitioners lie – you know, say they've got a girlfriend just to keep them quiet.

DOM: We're asking them to be truthful about themselves.

LIAM: Yeah.

DOM: So we have to be truthful.

LIAM: Not if it's not safe.

DOM: Mmmm.

LIAM: Well, the other thing we could do is ask for Brownie not to be brought down into the session.

DOM: Oh no, no.

LIAM: We could.

DOM: I didn't know I was going to find it this difficult.

LIAM: Think what a role model you are for these guys. You know, you're at college. You're making something of your life.

DOM: Yeah.

LIAM: That's why I wanted you on the project.

DOM: Don't like feeling like a freak, you know?

LIAM: You saying you don't want to carry on?

DOM: No.

LIAM: Right.

He looks at his watch again.

DOM: You got to go?

LIAM: I've got Zach tonight. Isy will kill me if I'm late picking him up.

DOM: Sorry.

LIAM: No, no.

DOM: I'll be alright.

LIAM: You sure?

DOM: Yeah.

LIAM: We can talk about it before the session tomorrow.

DOM: Yeah.

LIAM: If any time you feel uncomfortable, if Brownie says anything, I can always take him to one side. Or ask him to leave.

DOM: Yeah.

LIAM: Ok?

DOM: Yeah.

LIAM: See you tomorrow then.

DOM: Yeah, see you tomorrow.

SCENE SEVEN – VOICES 2

On the wing.

ASWAN is shouting.

ASWAN: I ain't done nothing. Let me see her. Sadie! I want to talk to her. Let me see her. Sadie!

BROWNIE: Shut up.

JAMAL: Aswan! What's wrong, blud?

DAMIAN: Aswan!

ASWAN: I just want to talk to her. Sadie!

BROWNIE: Shut up, I said.

JAMAL: You fucking shut up, Brownie. Aswan!

DAMIAN: Jamal! What's wrong with him?

JAMAL: Don't know.

ASWAN: Sadie!

BROWNIE: Sadie!

TOMMY: Sadie!

HASAN: Sadie!

They laugh.

SCENE EIGHT – ASWAN'S CELL

DAMIAN is listening to ASWAN. After a while TOMMY comes along and listens from outside the door.

ASWAN: She's sitting there and she's got my kid inside her and she's saying she don't want to see me no more. And there ain't nothing I can do about it because I'm in here and there's fucking guards all around us, you know? She says she's got to do the right thing for the baby and having a Dad who's in prison ain't going to exactly give it a good start in life. But that ain't Sadie saying that, that's her fucking Mother. Bitch. She's always had it in for me. She says her Mum is gonna go and live near Malaga and wants Sadie to go with her. That's fucking Spain I tell her. And I ask her if she's going to be getting back together with Ramon an all. He's this guy she knew over there when she went on holiday. And she says the trouble with me is that I always bring it down to to shit like that. And I says shit like what? And she says stuff about who's shagging who. So I tell her to fuck off and marry fucking Ramon. And she says that at least Ramon would be able to provide for a baby. And I tell her I don't see why my kid should have to put up with Ramon's dick coming in there when he's trying to get ready to be born. And she calls me a dickhead and I call her a fucking ho and she gets up to go, which is when I grab her round the throat. And the screws come up and twist my arm up my fucking back and the last thing I see is her walking out the door with my baby and she don't even look back when I tell her that I fucking love her and I want to see my kid. And I beg her not to do this to me. It's like I'm not fucking there. I'm just a piece of shit. I'm nothing.

Pause.

DAMIAN: You ain't nothing, man.

ASWAN doesn't respond. DAMIAN goes to look out the cell door. TOMMY goes into his cell before DAMIAN sees him.

DAMIAN: *(Returning.)* You want me to talk to someone?

ASWAN: What?

DAMIAN: It ain't like we ain't got friends on the outside. You could get some damage done to this girl.

ASWAN: I don't want no damage done to her. She's got my kid in her.

DAMIAN: We could get something done to this Ramon.

ASWAN: In fucking Spain!?

DAMIAN: You only have to say the word.

ASWAN: It won't bring her back.

SCENE NINE – THE THIRD CLASS

They are sitting in a circle playing a game. There is a good atmosphere in the room and laughter.

JAMAL is in the middle.

JAMAL: Everyone wearing trainers.

Everyone wearing trainers crosses the circle. DAMIAN is left out.

DAMIAN: Everybody who smokes.

Everyone crosses the circle except DOM, TOMMY and BROWNIE. OLU is left out.

OLU: Everyone who likes.....

BROWNIE: Sex.

OLU: Yes. Everybody who likes sex.

Laughter and hysteria. Everyone crosses the circle. TOMMY is left without a chair.

TOMMY: Everybody who watches Eastenders.

Everyone crosses except DOM and OLU. LIAM is left without a chair.

LIAM: Everyone who watches The Wire.

DOM crosses the circle. LIAM takes his seat.

DAMIAN: What's The Wire?

DOM: Everyone who supports Man U.

JAMAL stands. DOM takes his seat.

JAMAL: Shit man.

BROWNIE: You shouldn't support such crap.

JAMAL: Everyone who's got a kid.

LIAM: Good one.

Everyone changes places except DOM, ASWAN and HASAN.

JAMAL: *(Indicating HASAN.)* He didn't change places. Get up blud.

He tries to tip HASAN out of his chair.

BROWNIE: Fucking leave him alone.

DOM: Alright Brownie.

LIAM: Hasan, you've got a child so you have to change places.

HASAN stands up. He is terrified to be standing in the middle.

They all look at him and he tries to think of something to say.

LIAM: Anything. Something that's true for you.

JAMAL: Anyone who has to have protection.

LIAM: Jamal.

JAMAL: It's true. He has to have a screw take him from here to the wing.

LIAM: Let Hasan choose what he wants to say.

DAMIAN: Say something blud.

HASAN: Um…wearing trainers.

JAMAL: I said that.

HASAN: Ummmm –

DAMIAN: This is long man.

BROWNIE: Anyone who's an alcoholic, Liam.

LIAM: Thank you, Brownie. Come on, Hasan. Something about what you're wearing, your family…..

HASAN: Ummmm….

OLU: *(Getting up.)* I'll do it.

LIAM: Let him do it.

HASAN: Anyone who's in prison.

JAMAL: Fuck's sake!

BROWNIE: Nice one, Hasan.

All change. BROWNIE strolls up and deliberately makes sure he is last.

BROWNIE: Sit down! Anyone who's gay.

He looks pointedly at DOM as do some of the others.

LIAM: Hang on, hang on. Is this you coming out, Brownie?

BROWNIE: What?

LIAM: Are you saying you're gay?

BROWNIE: I ain't fucking gay.

LIAM: The rules are you have to choose something that's true for you. I thought, for a moment, you'd decided to be really brave there, Brownie.

BROWNIE: Alright. Anyone who's got a woman.

Everyone changes places apart from LIAM and DOM. ASWAN goes and sits at the side and doesn't join in.

LIAM: I've split up with my wife so I'm single at the moment.

BROWNIE: Dom didn't change places either.

DAMIAN has gone to talk to ASWAN. ASWAN has buried his head in his hands.

LIAM: You alright, Aswan?

JAMAL: He's feeling sick.

LIAM: Oh dear. You OK?

ASWAN: Yeah.

LIAM: You sure?

ASWAN: Yeah.

LIAM: OK. Let's see the scenes now, yeah? Get into groups.

DOM: Over here, Brownie, Tommy.

BROWNIE: We want Hasan in our group. Hey Hasan.

LIAM: No we need Hasan. So are we ready? Damian?

DAMIAN: Yeah?

LIAM: You ready to do the scene now?

DAMIAN: What scene?

LIAM: The one we were working on before the game. About what might stop you achieving your goals when you get out of here. What did your group choose, Dom?

BROWNIE: Going for a job and then they say they're going to phone you and they never fucking do.

LIAM: That's a good one, yeah.

OLU: That will not be a problem for me.

LIAM: No?

OLU: No. My uncle has a business. He will let me have a job any time. Any time.

LIAM: Well, some of us might not be so fortunate. And ours is about….? Anybody? What's ours about?

ASWAN: *(Still with his head in his hands.)* Family.

BROWNIE: What?

LIAM: They can't hear you, Aswan.

JAMAL: He said family.

LIAM: Say more about that.

ASWAN: Same people who judge you are the same people who love you.

BROWNIE: That's deep. Ain't it Tommy?

TOMMY doesn't say anything.

LIAM: So who's going first. Dom?

BROWNIE: You go first.

LIAM: OK.

DAMIAN: We're gonna act this, yeah?

LIAM: Yes, just like we rehearsed. Right! Get into position.

ASWAN: Come on little bro.

ASWAN slaps HASAN on the back as if he is being friendly but actually hits him hard.

ASWAN and JAMAL stand outside an imaginary front door. ASWAN presses the bell.

ASWAN: Ring, ring.

Nothing happens.

JAMAL: Liam. He's supposed to come to the door.

LIAM: What did we say about staying in character? Hasan, you have to open the door.

ASWAN: Start again. Start again. Ring, ring.

HASAN answers the door.

ASWAN: Hey little bro, how's it going?

He is deliberately roughing HASAN up.

JAMAL: Hey he's grown ain't he?

ASWAN: You remember my guy Jamal, don't you?

JAMAL: Wha gwarn little man? You got a 'tache there growing?

He pinches HASAN's face so LIAM enters to stop them.

LIAM: *(As MOTHER.)* Who is it?

ASWAN: It's me Mum.

Laughter from the others.

LIAM: Aswan?

ASWAN: Yeah Mum, I'm out of prison.

LIAM: Oh son, it's good to see you.

ASWAN: Yeah, but Mum, you didn't come to pick me up.

LIAM: Well, I wanted to darling, but I'd have had to come on the train.

ASWAN: It's ok. My man Jamal came to get me. You remember Jamal?

LIAM: Yes I remember him.

DAMIAN calls from inside the imaginary house.

DAMIAN: Who is it Eunice?

LIAM: It's nobody darling.

ASWAN: You what?

LIAM: It's just the Jehovah's Witnesses.

ASWAN: What's he doing here?

LIAM: Now, now, Aswan. He's a good man.

ASWAN: Why did you tell him it was the Jehovah's Witnesses? You not going to let me in?

LIAM: Well, I want to darling.

ASWAN: I come all the way over here to see ya.

LIAM: I know darling, it's lovely to see you, but it's not convenient.

ASWAN: Not convenient? What does that mean?

LIAM: We're about to go to Church darling.

ASWAN: Fuck that! It's that bastard. He don't want me here.

DAMIAN enters as Linton.

DAMIAN: What all the shouting about?

LIAM: It's nothing Linton, just go back to your telly.

DAMIAN: You!

LIAM: Linton!

DAMIAN: What does he want, Eunice?

LIAM: He just called to see us, Linton.

DAMIAN: Listen, Aswan, you nearly broke your mother's heart when you went to prison. You realise that?

ASWAN: That's none of your business.

DAMIAN: That's where you're wrong. It is my business. Your Mum and I are getting married.

ASWAN: Mum?

LIAM: I was going to tell you darling.

DAMIAN: So unless you show her that this time you're going to keep to the straight and narrow, she's decided she doesn't want anything to do with you.

ASWAN: That's my fucking Mum! He's my fucking brother.

DAMIAN: Mind your language please. And we don't want you coming round here with your jailbird friends corrupting him.

JAMAL: What's that supposed to mean?

DAMIAN: We don't want your brother going down the same road as Aswan.

JAMAL: Fuck you, man!

ASWAN: Jamal, let me handle this.

JAMAL: *(Threatening Linton.)* You're asking to get your head opened up.

DAMIAN: That's what I mean. Get off me doorstep before I call the police.

ASWAN: We ain't fucking done anything.

DAMIAN: Your friend just threatened me.

LIAM: Just calm down all of you.

ASWAN: I'm coming in.

DAMIAN: Over my dead body.

ASWAN: Let me in you tosser.

They start to struggle.

LIAM: Stop it! Stop it! Stop it!

The others stop fighting and look at LIAM/Eunice.

LIAM: Go back inside, Linton.

DAMIAN goes.

LIAM: *(To HASAN.)* And you.

HASAN goes.

LIAM: Perhaps it's best if you go, Aswan.

ASWAN: Mum!

LIAM: I'm sorry, darling.

LIAM mimes closing the door and goes. By this time ASWAN is fully in role emotionally.

ASWAN: Mum! Mum! Mum!

Silence. The others are impressed by his acting. JAMAL looks unsure what to do. He looks at LIAM.

JAMAL: That's it.

Applause. Hoots and whistles from DAMIAN.

ASWAN is wiping his eyes.

LIAM: You alright, Aswan?

ASWAN: Yeah.

He goes and sits down.

LIAM: Right. That was very emotional, wasn't it? So what do we learn from that?

DAMIAN: What do you mean?

LIAM: How could Aswan have responded differently?

BROWNIE: I think he should have mashed up Damian.

DAMIAN: I was Linton, man.

LIAM: OK, Brownie and what would that have achieved?

OLU: He was very good.

LIAM: Yes, he was good, but could he have done anything differently?

JAMAL: No, it was really believable.

LIAM: I don't mean what Aswan did wasn't believable – it was very believable. But could the character have behaved differently?

BROWNIE: /No.

TOMMY: /Maybe it's not in his nature to behave differently.

LIAM: Do you believe that Tommy?

TOMMY: What?

LIAM: That our actions are predestined because of who we are?

TOMMY: Maybe he's been through so much shit that he's never going to be able to react any different.

LIAM: Good point, very good point but what I'd like you to consider –

DOM: Uh Liam.....

LIAM: Yes?

DOM: They've come to take them back to the wing.

BROWNIE: Shit man, what about our scene?

LIAM: Sorry guys, they're early.

BROWNIE: They can fucking wait. Hey Guv, I'm just about to do some acting here!

LIAM: You know it doesn't work like that, Brownie. We'll do your scene tomorrow.

DAMIAN: Yeah, we'll see what sort of actors you and that nonce are, Brownie.

BROWNIE: Who you calling a nonce?

LIAM: Alright, you've done some great work today. Don't spoil it. See you tomorrow.

BROWNIE: See you Dom.

OLU: Ding Dom!

DOM: Yeah, see you.

SCENE TEN – VOICES 3

BROWNIE: Hey, Aswan! That was a fucking Oscar-winning performance!

JAMAL: Fuck off, Brownie.

BROWNIE: You going to start taking it up the arse now you're an actor?

Laughter from TOMMY, HASAN and OLU.

JAMAL: Why Brownie? You looking for another bitch?

DAMIAN: He's bored with you, Tommy!

JAMAL: He's got Hasan now.

DAMIAN: Hey Tommy! Fiddled with any kids lately?

BROWNIE: Shut the fuck up, crackhead!

JAMAL: Hey Hasan, there's some guys on C wing got beef with you. You're gonna get shanked, Hasan.

DAMIAN: Is it true you're a paedo, Tommy?

ASWAN: Tommy's a nonce!

BROWNIE: Hey Aswan! Mum! Mum! Let me in!

TOMMY and HASAN laugh.

BROWNIE: Mum! Mum!

HASAN/BROWNIE: Mum! Mum!

HASAN/BROWNIE/TOMMY: Mum! Mum! Mum!

They pretend to be crying loudly.

SCENE ELEVEN – THE FOURTH CLASS

BROWNIE: Go on, you interview me.

DOM: I think you guys should have a go first.

BROWNIE: No, you interview me.

DOM: I will later. But let's see one of you be the interviewer.

BROWNIE: Alright. Walk in the door then raghead.

OLU: Me?

BROWNIE: Yeah, come on.

(To DOM.)

What's your name?

DOM: Dom.

BROWNIE: Alright. My name's Dom.

OLU: I am Olufemi. I'd like a job please.

BROWNIE doesn't respond.

OLU: I am very hardworking. I will do anything. Well, not anything, but I want to work.

The others laugh at the very idea of OLU wanting to work.

OLU: *(Looking at JAMAL and DAMIAN.)* It's true!

JAMAL: Yeah yeah.

OLU: *(To BROWNIE.)* So can I have a job please?

BROWNIE: *(Suddenly.)* I'll call you.

He pushes OLU out the door.

OLU: My number! You take my number!

BROWNIE takes his number and tears it up.

LIAM: Alright. Yeah, that can happen.

BROWNIE: *(To DOM.)* Now you fucking interview me.

DOM: Tommy, don't you want a go?

BROWNIE: No, man, you interview me.

DOM: OK.

BROWNIE: Let me come in first.

BROWNIE enters. DOM holds out his hand and BROWNIE slaps it.

DOM: How was your journey in?

BROWNIE: It was alright.

DOM: OK. I've had a look at your CV and I was wondering if you can tell me what experience you've had that might help with this job.

BROWNIE: Are you serious?

DOM: Yes, I'm very serious.

BROWNIE: I come here to stack shelves and you wanna know what experience I've had?

DOM: Well, yes, there are a lot of people who want this job.

BROWNIE: A lot of people wanna stack fucking shelves?

DOM: Yes. Perhaps I could ask you to fill out a form with all your details.

BROWNIE: And then you'll call me, right?

DOM: Do you have any experience?

BROWNIE: Mopping floors in the nick.

DOM: Right.

BROWNIE: So you'll call me right?

DOM: Yes. I'll call you.

He holds out his hand and BROWNIE slaps it again.

BROWNIE: Your go, Tommy.

ASWAN: *(Under his breath.)* Fucking nonce.

BROWNIE: What you say?

TOMMY gets up.

DOM: Good morning. How was your journey in?

TOMMY: Is that relevant?

DOM: Pardon?

TOMMY: Is my journey here relevant to the job I'm being interviewed for?

BROWNIE: *(Laughing.)* You tell him, Tommy.

DOM: Well, I've looked at your CV. Could you identify some experiences which might stand you in good stead for the post?

ASWAN: *(Mimicking TOMMY.)* Well, I like to fiddle with little boys.

Laughter. During the next section there are responses from all the characters.

BROWNIE: What's so funny, huh? What's your fucking problem? What you gonna say on your CV?

ASWAN: Fuck off?

BROWNIE: What you gonna say on your CV? Go on tell us! That your woman's in fucking Spain with a guy called Ramon and that you're never going to see your kid again!

ASWAN: Hey! What the fuck's he talking about?

LIAM: Alright, sit down!

ASWAN goes for BROWNIE – a chair gets picked up.

LIAM: Sit down!

In the melee LIAM approaches the panic button. As soon as they see this the young men all stop fighting.

LIAM: Sit down, Brownie. Sit down or I press this.

The argument is still continuing.

LIAM: I'm going to press this unless you all sit down.

They all subside.

LIAM: Now you know as well as I do that I should have pressed this. You want me to press it? You want that? I press this, the guards come in and you get twisted up – in solitary – the lock up – forget it! What makes you think the rules don't apply in here, Brownie?

BROWNIE is whispering to TOMMY.

JAMAL: What's he saying to Tommy?

LIAM: It doesn't matter what people are saying. What should I do?

BROWNIE: Alright Liam.

LIAM: It's not alright though, is it? Some of you have said you want to see your kids on Friday. You want to be a proper father to them. And then this happens. So what? Is it all bullshit? Aswan?

ASWAN: Hey I didn't start nothing.

LIAM: Where does that get us? It's not about who starts it. We're looking at how you choose to respond to stuff that happens. Why are you here? What do you want to achieve here? What are you prepared to give up in order to get that? Why's everyone shouting one second and quiet the next? What do you want Jamal? Damian? What do you want Olu? Aswan? Brownie, what do you want?

BROWNIE: I want to see my fucking kid.

LIAM: And you think starting fights is a way to get to see Archie? I want to see my kid too. And if his mother pisses me off I don't fucking punch her.

DAMIAN: Language!

LIAM: You have to jump through a few hoops.

BROWNIE: Yeah but you leave here every day!

LIAM: Yeah I do. So what you gonna do to make sure that when you get out, you're not going to end up coming back?

DOM: *(Trying to calm things down.)* Alright –

LIAM: Thank you, Dom.

(To the lads.)

What do you want from this Brownie? I'm waiting for a proper answer.

BROWNIE: Ask fucking Aswan.

LIAM: No, I'm asking you. What do you want from this? Eh?

BROWNIE: I want to change.

Laughter.

LIAM: What's so funny?

JAMAL: He's a born fuckup, that's why.

LIAM: Do you want to change, Jamal?

JAMAL: This is shit.

LIAM: Oh is it? Great. Well you can always go back to the wing.

JAMAL: Yeah I want to. Where are the guards anyway?

LIAM: Is that how you all feel? You all want to give up?

Silence.

BROWNIE: You're just acting like a teacher, Liam.

LIAM: What else am I supposed to do when you all act like kids?

Silence.

TOMMY: How are we supposed to be any different?

LIAM: Go on.

TOMMY: You're talking like we're the ones with the power. What about the screws, the governor, the police, the government? Even if we change, they'll still treat us like shit.

LIAM: Focus on what you can change, rather than what you can't Tommy.

DAMIAN: This is long, man. I want to go back to my cell. It's less boring.

LIAM: *(Looking at his watch.)* Where are they? They're late. Listen, let's get back into a circle to finish.

JAMAL: I ain't getting in a circle.

BROWNIE: Fucking circle time.

LIAM: Don't then. But I'm going to finish off the session.

He moves his chair, as does DOM, and waits. The rest gradually make a circle.

BROWNIE: Alright, Dom?

DOM: I'm fine, Brownie.

LIAM: Look, there's been some very good work over the past couple of weeks. It's up to you whether you want to throw that away. So before we finish I wanted to set you something to do tonight.

JAMAL: I ain't doing shit!

LIAM: Don't do it then! Forget it. But for anyone who intends being here tomorrow I'd like to ask you to write a letter to your father or a father figure about how they made you feel as a kid. Maybe you think he made mistakes. If he did then tell him about it. Or maybe you want to thank him. Whatever. Yeah?

No response.

LIAM: Like I said, it's up to you.

DAMIAN: Sir?

LIAM: What?

DAMIAN: I can't do that.

LIAM: No? Why not?

DAMIAN: My Pops just moved here from Trinidad. I don't know his address.

LIAM: No, I don't mean.....you don't have to write a letter that you're going to send. I want you to write a letter saying all the things you'd really like to say but can't, just for yourself.

DAMIAN: But you ain't gonna send it?

LIAM: No.

DAMIAN: Oh right then.

LIAM: OK? Good. So for those of you that do want to come back, see you tomorrow.

SCENE TWELVE – TOMMY'S CELL

TOMMY is writing as BROWNIE dictates.

BROWNIE: I never understood why you were always pissing off and leaving us. I remember all them times Mum took me to see you in those places – going through them big gates and the guards searching Mum, running their fucking hands all over her. Searching my buggy. And I remember the smell of metal and concrete in that place. And sweat. And piss and shit. Then we'd go into this room and there'd be all these other men sitting there with their women and their kids. And Mum would tell me to go and sit on your lap and give you a kiss. And you'd push me away and tell me to put my fists up. And we'd pretend to box. And you'd make me cry because you always ended up punching me too hard. And when it came to time to leave I never understood why you weren't coming with us. And the men in suits would rattle their chains and take you away. Later when I did understand, there was always trouble on visiting days because I never wanted to go and see you. And Mum tried to make me. But I hated going there. I hated you for being in there. I didn't want to be in that place. Which is laughable seeing as how I've ended up in here with the smell of piss and shit and metal and concrete.

But I ain't you. I ain't gonna end up like you because you were a fucking loser.

Pause.

TOMMY: That it?

BROWNIE: Yeah.

TOMMY: Poetic.

BROWNIE: What?

TOMMY: The metal and the concrete and the way you come back to it at the end.

BROWNIE: Poetic?

TOMMY: Yeah.

BROWNIE: Shit.

TOMMY: It's like it's a vicious circle. No way out.

BROWNIE doesn't know what he feels about that.

TOMMY: That's what they want us to feel.

BROWNIE: What?

TOMMY: That there's no escaping who we are. They need us to stay like this. They want us to be deviant.

BROWNIE looks confused.

TOMMY: It's true. If they really wanted us to change why don't they rehabilitate us? Why don't they help us more when we get out? They need criminals so the rest of the population can feel normal.

BROWNIE: You saying I ain't normal?

TOMMY: It's like the State is the parent and we're the naughty children. And the more they tell us how naughty we are, the naughtier we become. We become what they tell us we are.

BROWNIE: Nobody tells me who I am.

TOMMY: In the past if you did something wrong you just got your hand cut off. Now what they do is put us in prison and make us feel like we're evil. They don't need to cut our hands off because we do it to ourselves. That's a much better way of controlling us. They make us ashamed of who we are.

BROWNIE: I ain't ashamed.

TOMMY: You're ashamed of your Dad.

BROWNIE: Fuck off, Tommy.

Pause.

BROWNIE: Give it here.

BROWNIE holds out his hand.

BROWNIE: Give it.

TOMMY hands him the letter. BROWNIE tears it up.

BROWNIE: It's bollocks. It's fucking bollocks. Ain't saying this shit in front of Jamal and Damian. No fucking way.

Pause.

BROWNIE: I ain't fucking ashamed.

He leaves.

SCENE THIRTEEN – ASWAN'S CELL

DAMIAN and JAMAL come to ASWAN's cell.

DAMIAN: Hey actor man!

ASWAN: Don't call me that.

JAMAL: The whole wing is talking about your acting, bruv.

DAMIAN: Even the screw was asking me about it.

JAMAL: Fucking Grandad came up to me in canteen and asked me if it was too late to join the class. He said he always wanted to be an actor.

DAMIAN: Plus he heard about things kicking off with Brownie and he wanted to get in on the action.

JAMAL: Fucking clown.

DAMIAN: You going to write a letter?

JAMAL: Fuck that.

DAMIAN: It's like school.

JAMAL: Yeah.

DAMIAN: Aswan?

ASWAN: What?

DAMIAN: You gonna write a letter?

ASWAN: I ain't going back to the class.

DAMIAN: Why not, bruv?

ASWAN: It's shit.

DAMIAN: But that scene's sick.

ASWAN: *(Aggressive.)* I ain't going back.

JAMAL: Why not?

ASWAN: Every fucker's laughing at me, calling me actor and shit.

DAMIAN: But you are an actor, man.

ASWAN: I'm not. I'm in this fucking nick and I got to live with these fuckers calling me "Oscar" and batty boy.

DAMIAN: You gotta come back, man.

ASWAN: Why?

DAMIAN: We can't do the scene without you.

ASWAN: Tough.

DAMIAN: But us three, we're tight. You're my guy.

ASWAN: I ain't your guy.

DAMIAN: Eh?

ASWAN: Leave it.

DAMIAN: What's up, man?

ASWAN: How did Brownie know all that stuff about Sadie?

DAMIAN: I don't know. Maybe someone in the family room heard what she was saying.

ASWAN: There weren't nobody near enough. Not to hear all them details about fucking Ramon and Spain and shit.

DAMIAN: What you saying, bruv?

ASWAN: I trusted you and you fucking backstab me.

DAMIAN: Oh my days, I never backstabbed you.

JAMAL: Listen, Aswan –

ASWAN: Fuck off out of my cell.

DAMIAN: Aswan? You serious?

JAMAL: It's Brownie, Aswan.

ASWAN: I know it's Brownie. But this snake has been chatting my business and now Brownie and all the fucking wing knows about it. As if the actor shit wasn't bad enough.

JAMAL: But if Damian said he ain't told nobody.

ASWAN: If he says that then he's lying!

DAMIAN: I'm not listening to this shit. You wanna know who your friends are Aswan.

ASWAN: I thought I did.

JAMAL: Damian. Damian!

DAMIAN goes.

JAMAL: Aswan, bruv.

ASWAN: Fuck off, Jamal.

JAMAL: This ain't right. You don't accuse your friends like that when you got no proof. You and Damian, you go back a long way.

ASWAN: That's what hurts.

JAMAL: Who you gonna believe? Your guy Damian? Or that fucker Brownie?

ASWAN: Damian tell you?

JAMAL: What?

ASWAN: Did he tell you about Sadie?

JAMAL: That ain't the point.

ASWAN: So he did tell you.

JAMAL: He told me because we're tight man.

ASWAN: Did you tell anyone?

JAMAL: Of course I fucking didn't. I wouldn't do that to you. And Damian wouldn't neither. You got the wrong guy.

ASWAN: Maybe.

JAMAL: *(Holding out his fist.)* Trust me.

ASWAN touches JAMAL's fist with his own.

SCENE FOURTEEN – BROWNIE'S CELL

BROWNIE: So what you saying, man?

HASAN: I'm just asking you, that's all.

BROWNIE: Tommy's alright.

HASAN: But there's all these rumours going round.

BROWNIE: You think I'd be friends with Tommy if he was a fucking paedo?

HASAN: No. But I got enough shit going on in here without that.

BROWNIE: What? So you want me to dump my guy just because some wankers are spreading rumours about him? That's not how Brownie works, man. That's not Brownie's way. Brownie's clever. You see how Aswan was looking at Damian at the end of that class? That was Brownie. Brownie will split up that fucking little love nest, just you watch. You come to Brownie if anyone's got beef with you.

HASAN: You ain't there all the time.

BROWNIE: What's the story with those guys in C wing?

HASAN: They're tramps, man.

BROWNIE: You know them?

HASAN: They know people I know in Canning Town.

BROWNIE: What did you do to upset them? I don't get it. There ain't no fucking smoke without fire. You told me you were in here for a bit of dealing. You go on their turf?

HASAN: No. I told you, they're tramps.

BROWNIE: So why do you need protection, man? Why you got the guards taking you everywhere when you go off the wing?

HASAN: I've told them I don't need that no more.

BROWNIE: Listen son, Brownie will look after you. People know that if they do anything to you, they got me to deal with. So stop listening to what those wankers are saying about Tommy and let's go and play some pool. OK?

HASAN: Yeah.

They leave BROWNIE's cell.

ASWAN and OLU are playing pool.

BROWNIE: Hey, raghead!

OLU: Brownie?

BROWNIE: Oooh, oooh, ahhh, ahh, ooohh, ooooh, oooh, fuck off. I want a word with Aswan.

OLU laughs it off.

BROWNIE: You don't mind if I butt in do you, Aswan?

ASWAN shrugs.

BROWNIE: *(To OLU.)* I thought I told you to fuck off.

OLU holds out his hands and goes.

BROWNIE: So, Aswan, how's it going?

ASWAN: Alright.

BROWNIE: Rack 'em up, Hasan.

HASAN racks the balls.

BROWNIE: That fucking Damian, innit?

ASWAN: What about him?

BROWNIE: He's got a big mouth, man.

ASWAN: That true?

BROWNIE: He smokes too many fucking drugs, know what I mean? He's all over the place, floating all over the place, chatting everybody's business.

ASWAN: You saying Damian told you about Sadie?

BROWNIE: Course he fucking did! How else would I know? He was telling everyone.

ASWAN: When?

BROWNIE: Yesterday in the showers. Like a fucking seminar. Go on mate, you break.

ASWAN breaks and starts to play.

BROWNIE: He said Sadie always was a fucking ho and you could never see it. This isn't me saying this, this is Damian mind. You should never trust a crackhead with your business, bruv.

JAMAL and DAMIAN enter.

JAMAL: Aswan!

BROWNIE: Shot man!

JAMAL: Hey Aswan! This the crowd you hanging out with now, then?

DAMIAN: Yo Aswan, let me catch up with you, blud.

BROWNIE: He don't want to talk to you. Fuck off.

DAMIAN: Aswan, man.

ASWAN: Fuck off, Damian.

JAMAL: Aswan.

ASWAN: Don't talk to me, man.

JAMAL: Why you listening to him, man? He's a fucking clown.

BROWNIE: This crackhead is the fucking clown. Chatting people's business in the shower.

DAMIAN: I wouldn't do that, Aswan.

BROWNIE calls to TOMMY who is in his cell.

BROWNIE: Hey Tommy!

TOMMY: *(From his cell.)* What?!!

JAMAL: *(To ASWAN.)* You really want to hang out with guys like this?

BROWNIE: Tommy, come here.

TOMMY: What you want?

BROWNIE: Come and tell us how we found out about Aswan's woman.

TOMMY: We heard Damian talking about it.

BROWNIE: Where?

TOMMY: In the showers.

JAMAL: You going to listen to this fucking nonce?

BROWNIE: And Tommy!

TOMMY: Yeah?

BROWNIE: What was that place in Spain where he said she was going?

TOMMY: Malaga.

BROWNIE: Like I said, Aswan, the guy's a fucking snake.

DAMIAN: Aswan this is shit.

ASWAN: Fuck off, Damian. You're a fucking snitch.

JAMAL and DAMIAN try to get to TOMMY. BROWNIE stands between them and him.

SCENE FIFTEEN – IN THE CELLS NIGHTTIME

The characters speak letters to their fathers – they are almost like dreams.

ASWAN: Dear Jarious Tate, it's your forgotten son, Aswan. Cynthia Richard's boy. Remember Cynthia? Thanks for all those birthdays when a card never came. Thanks for all those Christmases when my friends got bikes and I got a fucking Batman suit. Thanks for all the days when I came home from school and had to cook my own dinner because Mum was out cleaning to get enough money to bring up three kids on her own. Thanks for her aching feet and bad back. Thanks for her tiredness and rages. Thanks for the beatings she gave me when she couldn't take no more. Dear Jarious Tate, thanks for nothing.

HASAN: Bro, you're the nearest thing I got to a Dad. You always said you'd look after me but in the last few years you weren't around too much. You were my big brother, my hero, but then you weren't there no more. You had your women, your job, your car and it felt like you didn't need me no more. It felt like nobody in that house gave a fuck what I was doing. So I went out and found other brothers. They cared about me. My bredren. People my own age who understood what it felt like to be me. That was my fam. They made me feel like I mattered.

TOMMY: I'm three or four years old and I'm sitting in your lap watching a video. And I'm scared cos Shere Khan is creeping up on Mowgli but I feel safe on your lap protected from everything. You tell me you remember going to see The Jungle Book in the cinema with your Dad and you sing along to all the songs. "I wanna be like you-oo." I can hear your voice making your chest vibrate – it's like there's an engine in there, purring away. And Shere Khan the tiger is licking his lips and looking hungrily at Mowgli – he's getting ready to pounce and you hold me tight as I wriggle with fright. I can feel the roughness of your chin against my cheek – you smell of sweat and cigarette smoke. Will Baloo get there in time to save Mowgli? You have thick black hairs on your arm and I ask you if I'll get hairs like that one day. You tell me I will and I stroke your arm – it feels like fur. On the video Baloo rescues Mowgli from the tiger and Shere Khan slinks off into the jungle. But you're not watching any more. You're looking at me. It's like you're shining a spotlight on me. I feel special and loved.

DAMIAN: Pops, I can still remember the trip to the airport. You cussing at the traffic and Mums worried we were going to miss our plane. I remember having my first taste of a McDonald's while we waited for our flight. Mums and you weren't saying nothing and I didn't understand then what I do now. You both knew you wouldn't be coming over to join us in England even though you pretended that you were. It's funny Pops, in my mind I can see you standing on the runway and waving to us as we took off. Mums says no way can that have happened. She said you didn't even wait for us to get on the plane. But in the cold, in the winter, in Peckham, I held on to that memory – of the heat and the sunlight and you standing there getting smaller and smaller until you were just a speck on that little island in the big blue ocean.

JAMAL: Your violent temper and your fucking fists – that's what I remember most about you. And the fear we all felt when you were in the house. And knowing that after you'd beat up Mum you'd start on us. Just because you could. The fucking mad thing was that I missed you when I was put in care. All I wanted was to be home. I made sure that no foster family every wanted to keep me for long. I didn't want no other family. I kidded myself that maybe things would be different if I was back with you all. But I never got the chance to find out, did I? But there's one thing I'd like to thank you for. You gave me a good preparation for being in here. Cos every fucker in here is trying to be like you. Getting violent for no reason and lashing out – hiding what they're feeling inside. That house was a good training for prison – it stopped you expecting men to know about anything like kindness or love.

OLU: I thought you were a king, my father. A king among men. From a line of kings. Your ancestors were kings and they were watching over us. I could not believe it that in England people did not see that you were a king. I remember I was on my way home from school and I saw you in your uniform on the other side of the road. You were giving a parking ticket to a man in a big car. He was shouting at you and calling you bad names. I thought why does my father not call on Ogun to destroy this man with his sword? Instead you said nothing. The man tore up the parking ticket and threw it in your face. You turned your back and pressed the buttons on your meter reader. The man tried to drive his car over you and you had to jump back. And across the street I hid in a shop until you had gone. That was when I stopped believing that the ancestors were watching over us.

BROWNIE: Standing in the rain with Mum at your grave. I didn't feel nothing. Nothing. The priest talked about you returning to the arms of our Lord and I remember thinking that you'd probably headbutt the Lord if he tried to put his arms around you. He talked about how sometimes it seems like life is too hard to bear and how sometimes we don't feel strong enough to carry on but how the Lord is testing us. Well you failed that test, you loser. All you could do was tie your sheet in a noose and put it round your neck. I'd say you got nought out of ten for that answer.

SCENE SIXTEEN – THE FIFTH CLASS

Everyone apart from ASWAN is sitting in the circle (OLU next to DOM). LIAM has just asked them who wants to read out their letter. They all look at the floor shiftily.

Silence.

LIAM: Jamal?

No response.

LIAM: Damian?

No response.

LIAM: Aswan? Oh, where is Aswan?

No response.

LIAM: Damian?

DAMIAN: Yeah?

LIAM: Where's Aswan?

DAMIAN: How should I know, Sir?

(To BROWNIE.)

What you looking at, bruv?

BROWNIE: Just looking.

LIAM: Well anyone else? Tommy?

BROWNIE: Nobody wants to read out shit like that, Liam. It's personal.

DOM: Shall I go first?

LIAM: No, I don't think that's – you've written one?

DOM: Yes.

LIAM: No, I don't think that's appropriate.

BROWNIE: Why not?

LIAM: Because this isn't for us. This is for you guys.

BROWNIE: Yeah, but if Dom's written a letter, we should hear it. Go on, Dom.

LIAM: No, I –

BROWNIE: I wanna hear Dom's letter.

LIAM and DOM look at each other. LIAM is pretty cross that DOM has sprung this on him.

LIAM: OK.

DOM: Yeah?

LIAM: Yeah, ok.

DOM gets out a piece of paper.

DOM: Dear Dad, during my childhood you were the most loving and caring father anyone could have asked for.

Silent looks between the group. DAMIAN laughs and whispers to JAMAL.

DOM: You were always there for me and I knew that if you punished me then there was a good reason for it. You never lashed out in anger. You only ever smacked me once – Aunty Doreen's broken vase – and I remember thinking that it hurt you more than the physical pain hurt me. When I heard about my friends' relationships with their Dads I felt very lucky to have a father like you.

JAMAL: *(Under his breath.)* It's a fucking love letter.

DOM: The downside of this was that I've probably ended up caring too much about what you think of me. It was hard sometimes to be myself around you. I didn't want your disapproval. As time went on I made certain realizations about myself. I felt more and more that I was lying to you. So in the end, after much soul-searching, I told you things that you would probably have preferred not to know. Now we are not talking to each other and I sometimes wish I had not been so honest. I love you Dad and I know that whatever you say, you love me too. I hope that you will realize that, this time at least, you have made a mistake and that one day you will be able to accept me for who I am. Love Dom.

Pause.

OLU: Ding Dom!

Laughter.

LIAM: Good.

BROWNIE: Who are you, Dom?

DAMIAN: So you not talking to your Dad?

LIAM: Let's move on.

DOM: No, I'm not.

JAMAL: Why not?

DOM: He doesn't approve of my lifestyle.

BROWNIE: You mean, you're gay?

LIAM: Brownie I don't think that's anybody's business but D –

DOM: Yes I am. Gay. And when I told my Dad, he threw me out.

Uproar in the room. OLU picks up his chair and gets as far away from DOM as possible.

OLU: I'm not sitting there.

BROWNIE: *(Triumphant.)* I said it. I fucking said it.

OLU: That's disgusting.

LIAM: Alright, alright, calm down.

OLU: Nooo! I was sitting right beside him! Noooo!

LIAM: Alright, Olu.

OLU: Nooooooooo!

The others find his reaction hilarious.

LIAM: Alright, calm down.

DAMIAN: Your father threw you out on the street?

DOM: Yeah.

DAMIAN: Shit. So where you living?

DOM: Well…ummm…

He hesitates.

DAMIAN: What? With your boyfriend?

DOM: Yes.

OLU: NOOOOOOOOO!

More hilarity at OLU's response.

LIAM: OK. Thank you, Dom, for being so honest. Who's next? Brownie?

BROWNIE: I ain't reading out a letter.

DOM: Why not?

LIAM: I don't think anybody should be forced.

DOM: You not man enough?

LIAM: Dom!

BROWNIE: Fuck off.

DAMIAN: *(To DOM.)* You know? Respect man.

The others look at him surprised.

DAMIAN: I got one.

He unfolds his letter.

DAMIAN: Yeah, Pops, they say better late than never. You did come back into my life too late to stop me doing stuff that got me in trouble. But when I saw you in the courtroom, I felt all sorts of things. I felt ashamed that you were hearing about tings I'd done that I'm not proud of; I felt angry that you hadn't been there until then; but most of all I felt that somebody cared what happened to me, Pops. And when I was sent down I didn't feel nothing till I looked at your face and there were tears in your eyes, man. Real tears.

BROWNIE: Boo hoo.

DAMIAN: You got a problem, friend?

LIAM: Carry on, Damian.

DAMIAN: Pops you say you're going to be there for me and I know now what I've been missing. When I'm out of the lockdown I want to make up for some of the mistakes I've made. But the most important thing is, I want to make sure Connor doesn't have to go without a father like I had to for so many years.

BROWNIE: Touching.

DAMIAN: I'm not even talking to you, man.

DAMIAN sits down.

LIAM: Anyone else?

OLU: Me. I'll go.

LIAM: OK.

OLU gets up. He has not written his letter and is making it up on the spot.

OLU: Yes, Father. You are a great man and I love you very much. You were very sad when I came to prison but I want to tell you that when I get out, I will make a lot of money so that you do not have to work. And I will buy you a big house and give you many grandchildren.

(To LIAM.)

Is this good?

LIAM: I don't know, Olu. Is it good for you?

OLU: Huh?

LIAM: I asked you if it was good for you.

OLU: Yes, I think it is very good.

He sits down.

BROWNIE: Fucking bollocks.

LIAM: So anyone else? Tommy?

TOMMY shakes his head.

LIAM: Hasan, what about you?

BROWNIE: We ain't doing it.

LIAM: OK.

JAMAL: Yeah, I'll do mine.

He gives BROWNIE a stare.

LIAM: Great, Jamal.

BROWNIE: This I must hear.

JAMAL: It ain't very long, Liam.

LIAM: That's alright.

JAMAL: *(Looking at BROWNIE.)* Dear scumbag, go fuck yourself! Yours sincerely, Jamal.

BROWNIE: Now that's a letter.

JAMAL: Yeah? At least I know how to write.

BROWNIE: That's a fucking letter.

LIAM: Fair enough. Sometimes there's a lot of anger that needs expressing. Good. Do we know if Aswan has written anything?

No response.

LIAM: Right. So that's everyone.

HASAN: Uhh….Liam.

LIAM: Hasan?

HASAN: I wrote something.

JAMAL and DAMIAN smile.

DAMIAN: Yes, my man!

HASAN: It's not to my Dad. It's to my brother.

LIAM: That's fine.

HASAN: Dear Mehmet. He's called Mehmet.

LIAM: Fine.

HASAN: I'm writing to you to ask you something. You knew I was carrying a shank. You saw it in my pocket and you never said nothing. Mum didn't know, but you did. You could of told me not to be so stupid. You could of told Mum. You could of stopped me going out the door tooled up. That would have been looking after me. Instead you pretended you hadn't seen nothing. Now there's two families who have lost a son. Me and the person I killed.

Response from DAMIAN and JAMAL particularly.

OLU: He killed someone!

LIAM: OK, Olu, calm down.

HASAN: I wish it hadn't happened but it has. And I'm going to take my punishment for as long as it takes. But when I do get out, I hope I can be a better guide for my child than you have been for me. Your brother Hasan.

DAMIAN: Shit, bruv, how long you in for?

LIAM: Damian! Thank you, Hasan. I appreciate that it must have taken a lot of courage to say that here.

JAMAL and DAMIAN clap and LIAM, DOM and OLU join in.

The clapping dies down.

BROWNIE: Someone's found their fucking voice.

SCENE SEVENTEEN – THE POOL TABLE

ASWAN and OLU are playing pool. JAMAL and DAMIAN are watching from a distance. ASWAN is deliberately ignoring them.

OLU: It is murder. He will be in prison for a long time.

ASWAN: Guv says twenty years.

OLU: Twenty years. He will be an old man when he leaves this place.

HASAN comes out of his cell.

ASWAN: *(Seeing HASAN.)* Shut up! Your shot.

He hands the cue to OLU.

OLU: Hey Hasan, you want to play pool with us?

ASWAN: We haven't finished this game.

OLU: Hasan is my friend.

ASWAN: Yeah? Since when?

OLU: Come my friend and play pool.

DAMIAN: *(To OLU.)* We're on next, blud.

JAMAL: Hey Hasan. All the clowns in this place want to be your friend now.

ASWAN: Who you calling a clown?

JAMAL: I didn't mean you, bruv.

ASWAN: *(To OLU.)* You playing or what?

OLU lines up his shot.

JAMAL: So, Hasan, where's your little crew today?

HASAN: Who?

JAMAL: Who? Brownie and the nonce. Something should be done about that nonce, man. We got our families coming tomorrow.

DAMIAN: What you saying, bruv?

JAMAL: How you feeling about Tommy being in the same room with our kids? What if he tries it on with one of them?

DAMIAN: You serious, man?

JAMAL: How old's your kid again?

HASAN: A month old.

JAMAL: All the same.

OLU: But I have four children!

JAMAL: They're all coming?

OLU: Yes of course.

JAMAL: 'Kin hell!

OLU: I'll kill him if he goes near my child. I don't care what happens to me.

ASWAN: This is bullshit. Tommy ain't a nonce.

JAMAL: How do you know?

HASAN: He's pretty weird, man. Don't understand half the stuff that he and Brownie chat about.

DAMIAN: Why you hanging with clowns like that?

HASAN: I'm not.

JAMAL: But Brownie's your guy, right?

HASAN: Wouldn't say that.

JAMAL: Right.

HASAN: I don't mind Brownie. It's Tommy.

OLU: I'll kill him.

HASAN: Brownie won't do anything without asking Tommy about it first.

JAMAL: Yeah?

HASAN: He's sneaky too. Always listening and shit and then telling Brownie about it afterwards.

DAMIAN: Listening?

HASAN: Yeah. Tommy heard you and Aswan talking about Aswan's girl. He was standing outside the cell. Went straight back and told Brownie about it.

JAMAL: Raaaaaaa!

HASAN: So then they made up the story about Damian chatting about it in the showers.

DAMIAN: Fucking tramp!

ASWAN has stopped playing.

HASAN: I swear if Tommy asked Brownie to suck his dick, Brownie would do it.

BROWNIE has entered.

BROWNIE: Hasan!

HASAN turns.

BROWNIE: Coming gym?

HASAN: Not today, Brownie. Got a bad back.

BROWNIE: Yeah? You wanna be careful playing pool. All that bending over.

HASAN: OK.

BROWNIE looks at them for a moment and goes.

HASAN: Give my love to Shirley!

The others laugh. ASWAN and DAMIAN clasp hands.

JAMAL: Who the fuck's Shirley?

SCENE EIGHTEEN – TOMMY'S CELL

TOMMY: I just think it took a lot of guts.

BROWNIE: So what you saying?

TOMMY: What?

BROWNIE: That I ain't got guts?

TOMMY: No.

BROWNIE: That's what he was saying. He said I wasn't man enough to read out my letter. The guy's a battyman.

TOMMY doesn't say anything.

BROWNIE: What is all this Tommy?

TOMMY: I want to read out a letter.

BROWNIE: You what?

TOMMY doesn't say anything.

BROWNIE: We agreed. We're not reading out our letters.

TOMMY: I know.

BROWNIE: What's it going to look like?

TOMMY doesn't say anything.

BROWNIE: This isn't about having guts. It's about being gutless. You think if you tell them what you did, that will stop them calling you a nonce? They don't work like that Tommy. Anything they find out about you they use against you. It will make it worse.

TOMMY: Maybe.

BROWNIE: What happened to all that talk about not caring what anyone thinks about you? About being your own fucking person?

TOMMY: It's easy to say. Lot harder to do.

BROWNIE: So you're ratting me out.

TOMMY: No.

BROWNIE: That's what it looks like to me. In here, you're either for me or against me.

TOMMY: Doesn't have to be like that.

BROWNIE: Oh doesn't it? I'll be the only one who hasn't read his letter. Jamal will be crowing.

TOMMY: You could read yours out too.

BROWNIE: I ain't reading out no letter to my fucking Dad. You hear me? You fucking snake. I'm telling you, you ain't going to read out that letter.

TOMMY: And I'm telling you that I am.

BROWNIE: Then you can take the consequences Tommy. Don't say I didn't warn you.

SCENE NINETEEN – VOICES 4

JAMAL: Hey Brownie, is it true? Brownie?

DAMIAN: Is what true?

JAMAL: Grandad said Tommy went on the internet pretending to be a little kid. That's why he's in here.

OLU: Tommy, Tommy, Tommy!

DAMIAN: Say that again.

JAMAL: Tommy goes looking for kids on the internet and pretends to be a kid himself.

OLU: Tommy I'm going to kill you.

ASWAN: How does Grandad know that?

JAMAL: Someone told him, didn't they Brownie?

DAMIAN: Who told him?

JAMAL: Who told him Brownie? Brownie and his girlfriend have split up.

DAMIAN: Thought Brownie's girlfriend was a skipping rope! What's her name, Hasan?

HASAN: Shirley!

Laughter from OLU, ASWAN, JAMAL and DAMIAN.

JAMAL: So now Brownie's dishing the dirt on Tommy. You gonna sell his story to the Sun, Brownie?

DAMIAN: What happened Brownie? Did Tommy get tired of telling all those porkies for you?

JAMAL: No Brownie's too old for Tommy. Hey! Tommy! You'd better not show up at drama tomorrow. We don't want you anywhere near our kids.

ASWAN: You'd better watch yourself Tommy if Brownie hasn't got your back no more.

OLU: Tommy, Tommy, Tommy!

JAMAL: You're going to get shanked, Tommy.

OLU: I'm going to kill you Tommy.

JAMAL starts a chant

JAMAL: Nonce, nonce, nonce!

The others join in one by one, first OLU, then HASAN, then DAMIAN, then ASWAN and finally BROWNIE. TOMMY sits in his cell listening.

SCENE TWENTY – IN THE CHAPEL

OLU, JAMAL, BROWNIE and HASAN are lined up at the back of the stage. DOM and LIAM at either end. They are watching DAMIAN and ASWAN slowly move towards each other. DAMIAN is the Father and ASWAN is the Son. They have not seen each other for ten years. The only words they are allowed to use are "Dad" from ASWAN and "Son" from DAMIAN.

There is dead silence from the watchers.

The scene will change depending on the impulses of each performance.

DAMIAN: Son?

ASWAN looks at him.

DAMIAN moves closer.

DAMIAN: Son!

ASWAN steps back keeps eye contact.

DAMIAN: Son.

They look at each other.

After a pause DAMIAN moves closer.

DAMIAN: Son.

This time ASWAN doesn't move so DAMIAN moves closer.

DAMIAN: Son.

ASWAN is on the verge of tears.

DAMIAN moves closer.

DAMIAN: Son.

He touches ASWAN. ASWAN moves his shoulder but does not step away. After a moment DAMIAN touches him again.

DAMIAN: Son.

ASWAN looks at him.

DAMIAN: Son.

Eventually they embrace.

ASWAN: Dad, Dad, Dad.

LIAM and DOM start clapping and the others join in. The boys take a bow. The real audience might well think this is the end of the play.

LIAM steps forward and halts any applause.

LIAM: Thank you everyone for coming. Working on this project has been amazing. The young men that you see up here have been very courageous in sharing their experiences, their stories, their lives with each other and now with you as an audience. Because everything that you've seen in the last hour has come from them in one way or another. At times I have to say it has been challenging but I hope both you and they will agree that it has felt worth it.

As he speaks the cast start to relate to their families from where they're standing on the stage. DAMIAN starts this by waving at Connor. Maybe there are little mimed conversations between them and their girlfriends etc.

LIAM: But before we finish I'd just like us to remember that this project has been about transformation – If you can just hang on guys –

DOM: Guys.

LIAM: I know you've got people in the audience that you're eager to talk before you have to go back to the wing.

He talks to a guard at the back of the audience.

LIAM: What time do they have to go back to the wing? OK. So we wanted to give the last word to Damian.

DAMIAN is engrossed in relating to Connor and his father.

LIAM: Damian?

DAMIAN: Yeah?

LIAM: There was something you were going to say?

DAMIAN: Yeah.

DAMIAN looks at his family member and Connor.

LIAM: Go on, then.

DAMIAN: What? Oh right yeah. I just wanted to say from my heart, you know, thanks to Liam and Dom. Doing this acting thing and all the other stuff has made me really think, you know, about who I am and what I want for my kid. I'm looking at my boy there and I'm seeing my Pops there in the audience holding him, and I'm feeling that maybe, you know, I can change. Things can change. So yeah. Yeah.

DOM leads applause followed by ASWAN, JAMAL, LIAM, OLU and HASAN.

LIAM: Right so thank you. I'm going to let you all have some time with your families now.

The boys (all except ASWAN.) advance on the audience – lighting change as they do. They hold out their arms to their children and mime responding to them. It is gentle and touching and tender and we see them in a completely different light. Music.

SCENE 21 – CODA: THE LAST SESSION

The following Monday. Evaluation. They are sitting in a circle. TOMMY is the only one not present.

LIAM: Jamal?

JAMAL: My word would be strength. Like strength through knowing yourself. I never thought I could stand up in front of people like that and I'm definitely going to keep writing.

LIAM: Yeah, they liked your lyrics.

JAMAL: So it's made me feel strong knowing I can do that.

LIAM: Hasan?

HASAN: Can I have two words?

LIAM: Alright.

HASAN: The first one's regret.

LIAM: OK.

HASAN: And the other one's hope.

LIAM: Good.

OLU: That was my word. I wanted to say hope.

LIAM: You can have hope too, Olu.

OLU: I want to have my own word,

LIAM: OK.

LIAM looks at his watch. OLU thinks.

LIAM: Shall we come back to you?

OLU: No. No. OK, I'll have hope.

LIAM: Good. Aswan.

ASWAN: Yeah, you know it's been a difficult time for me. But it's made me think there's something I can do. I was never any good at anything. And this class has made me feel like this acting thing is something I can do. When I get out of here I'm going to see if maybe it's something I could follow up like.

LIAM: I could certainly help you with that.

OLU: You going to go to Hollywood, Aswan?

JAMAL: Raaaa!

DAMIAN: Sir, are you going to come back and teach us some more?

LIAM: I don't know about that.

ASWAN: I just want Sadie and my baby to know that I'm worth something you know. I've written to her and tried to explain to her like that I want to make something of myself.

LIAM: Have you heard back?

ASWAN: Not yet. So yeah, my word is self-respect.

LIAM: OK. Brownie.

DOM: Liam.

DOM whispers to LIAM that TOMMY is outside waiting to come in. DOM goes.

LIAM: Right. We've just got Brownie and Damian. Brownie?

BROWNIE: My word's trust.

LIAM: You've learnt to trust.

BROWNIE: I've learnt how important it is to be able to trust people.

LIAM: Right. And Damian.

DAMIAN: One word? I don't think one word, can do justice to it. Like I said on Friday, it's made me really think.

LIAM: The word you used was change.

DAMIAN: Yeah. That's right. We gave you a hard time Liam – and you Dom. We didn't always like treat you with respect. But you really stuck with us. And we really respect you. And I think we have all changed. We've learnt not to diss each other all the time and to respect each other.

DOM returns with TOMMY. TOMMY has clearly been beaten up and has blood on his T-shirt.

OLU: Nonce. You don't come in here.

JAMAL: Go and find yourself a kiddy to fiddle with.

The others jeer and join in.

DAMIAN: What's he doing here, Sir?

LIAM: Hang on, Hang on. So this is how you've changed is it? Damian?

DAMIAN: Sir, this ain't right.

LIAM: One minute you're talking about respect and the next you're behaving like this. Tommy is part of this group and he wants to read us something. Is that right Tommy?

TOMMY: Yeah.

JAMAL: *(Under his breath.)* I ain't listening to this.

LIAM: Go ahead, Tommy.

TOMMY: To my father.

JAMAL: Shit.

TOMMY: The man who made me feel powerless, dirty, shameful.

JAMAL: 'Cos you fucking are.

LIAM: Jamal.

TOMMY: Two years ago I became a father myself. And I felt this rage at you for what you did to me. It was like I'd never understood it until then. The thought of anyone doing to Emily what you did to me made me feel sick. I couldn't stop thinking about it. It wasn't me that was dirty and shameful. It was you. And out there, there were other people like you. Men looking for children. I got obsessed. Every night I was on the internet, surfing chatrooms. I called myself the Jungle Boy and I said I was nine years old. And then someone took the bait. A man like you. He told me where to meet him and I went. He wasn't old, or bald or fat. He looked normal. Like you. But I knew what he wanted. I was going to stop him ever doing to a child what you did to me. As I kicked him, I imagined it was you. I imagined that the blood on my boot was your blood. His screams were your screams. And when I got my sentence, I didn't feel any remorse. Justice had been done.

They all look at TOMMY and he looks back. The lights slowly fade.

www.ingramcontent.com/pod-product-compliance
Lightning Source LLC
LaVergne TN
LVHW020657100826
845148LV00012B/2531

* 9 7 8 1 8 4 9 4 3 0 2 3 4 *